COLLECTED POEMS

Rainer Brambach

COLLECTED POEMS

Translated by Esther Kinsky

LONDON NEW YORK CALCUTTA

swiss arts council

pr⊃helvetia

This publication has been supported by a grant from
Pro Helvetia, Swiss Arts Council

Seagull Books, 2014

Originally published as *Gesammelte Gedichte* by Rainer Brambach
© Diogenes Verlag AG, Zurich, 2003

Illustrations in 'Also in April' by Tatjana Hauptmann © Diogenes
Verlag AG, Zurich

English Translation © Esther Kinsky, 2014

ISBN 978 0 8574 2 171 5

Typeset by Seagull Books, Calcutta, India
Printed and bound by Maple Press, York, Pennsylvania, USA

Contents

Also in April

←

Rainer Brambach, who was born in 1917 and died in 1983, had an unusual life as a poet. The child of a Swiss mother and a German father, he grew up in Basel, left school at the age of 14 to be apprenticed to a house painter and took up various manual jobs. As a German national, he was deported to Germany at the outbreak of the Second World War but returned illegally and spent the following years in hiding and, after he was apprehended, in a prison and a labour camp in Switzerland. The experience of being an outcast and prisoner left its mark on him and is repeatedly referred to with defiant pride in his writing. After the war, Brambach published a few small collections of poetry which were printed and circulated by friends and supporters, and eventually attracted the attention of a major publisher in Switzerland as well as the editors of influential literary periodicals in West Germany. Literary recognition and awards notwithstanding, Brambach remained an outsider who continued to earn most of his living as a labourer, building roads, gardening, cutting stone as a stonemason's assistant, and mingling with the precarious *bohème* of Basel. Forever unwilling to subscribe to conventions, Brambach lived for many years in poverty, preferring the solitary walker's and casual labourer's freedom to the constraints associated with a more comfortable life. Disregard for material values, a profound engagement with the landscape of the Upper Rhine and a lasting commitment to humane concerns shaped his poetry. At the same time, he was deeply literate, well read in poetry of all ages, as the references and quotes in his own work betray and, as his friend and mentor Hans Bender wrote in a brief afterword to Brambach's *Collected Poems*, a great admirer of many of his contemporaries.

Brambach left a small *oeuvre*. The 140 poems which constitute this collection—most of them short—were published in two volumes, *Toss a Coin* and *Also in April*, which he edited. Brambach didn't live to see the latter volume published; he died shortly after completing his work on the selection. According to his friends, he destroyed a number of earlier poems which he no longer liked, and no printed version of these early works seems to have survived. Regardless of his relatively small output and the life he led far from urban intellectual and literary circles, Brambach was much appreciated by his colleagues like Hans Magnus Enzensberger and Günther Eich. When I recently met the Swiss writer and artist Erica Pedretti, her face lit up at the mention of Rainer Brambach's name, and she was eager to share memories of her encounters with this 'wonderful poet and person'.

Brambach was a poet outside of all fashion, and the reader will soon recognize his peculiar and specific tone—direct, unadorned, free of any pomp, but also of ideology and political message. His quiet and unspectacular images conjure up a landscape, a small rural scene, the interior of a bar or a cafe, and offer a glimpse into a depth of meaning suddenly and briefly opening up to the beholder. Brambach was, above all, an observer, most at home when finding the words to describe a landscape in a particular light, a particular mood and weather. As a poet, he took to the visual world like a gardener to a natural space or a stone-mason to a block of sandstone—immediately recognizing the shape, the expression, the message hidden beneath the surface of the untreated matter. His writings provide insights of deceptive simplicity. Nevertheless, they form a poetic essence that will hopefully resonate in the minds of those who read this volume.

Esther Kinsky
Berlin, June 2012

Toss a Coin

LIFE

I write no business letters,
I don't insist on a delivery date
nor ask for an extension.
I write poems.

I write poems at fairgrounds,
in museums, barracks and zoos.
I write wherever
people and animals grow alike.

I've dedicated many poems to the trees.
Upon which they grew up to the sky.
Who will dare to deny
that these trees did not grow up to the sky?

Not one line to death, so far.
I weigh eighty kilos, and life is mighty.
Some other time he'll come and ask,
What about the two of us?

LUMBERJACK BAR

In the bar a row of bottles,
lumberjacks in bearlike coats,
firwood benches notched by axes
and the stove that hums a song.

Stubby pipes and sawdust floor
stained with black tobacco marks—
Taste the smell of pine on loden
touch the bread in the bag of jute

Move closer to the fire and listen
to the charcoal burner's tale,
you'll see kilns and smoke-like figures,
and in the wood a resin face.

Tunes of winter, smoke and legends,
and the burden of loneliness
which you bear through breaks in forests
in snow blind, wood crazed, struggling on.

THE GREENHOUSE, MY ABODE

Sitting under palm fronds, what would I see
outside?—Frozen compost, the empty
truss of chestnut trees along the avenue, nothing living
apart from some crows.

The battered watering can, the frayed
straw hat and a pair of worn-out boots
remind me kindly
of summer's daily labour.

The heater's humming. Snow is falling on the glass roof.
I am a happy tenant, surrounded by
my friends with Latin names.
The cacti though are closest to my heart.

MARCH IN BASEL

Whatever March may hold in store, all gardens
have agreed to blossom.
Don't hesitate, cast the ashes
left behind by winter on the wind.

Whoever lost his glove in the snow
won't grieve for it any more.
Whoever is wearing the fool's garb,
whistling askance as he comes home in the morning,
will see the moon as a swollen pig's bladder.

Whatever March holds in store, do not
the doubter heed!
The blackbird escaped the frost, hark its song!

SNOW

The sky is pouring out snow
The crows prove themselves black on white
The calendar says: May
We say: Gorse, jasmine,
firebush, sloe, forsythia
We clear the garden paths
wondering if this is the end of it all
forever—
Snow—the falling answer.

IN THOSE TIMES

In those times of which I tell you
I dug earth and ate my bread by the fence,
wore a coarse shirt, corduroy pants and Garibaldi hat
and blew my nose into my empty hand.

It rained in March, bad-tempered
I shovelled earth and stood
deep in the ditch in August, eyes down,
silent thunderstorms of dust above.

Some eight storeys deeper than the mole
I dug the pickaxe in the gravel with full force.
Cold glowed a fire in the stone and sparks were flying
against the wooden mould.

Snow covered the earth bank when they laid the cables—
December and a sky as of cement
The only thing that offered comfort was the roll-up,
the Burrus Bleu and its leathery smell.

DAY'S LABOUR

He who cycles to the quarry before dawn
and from the quarry after dusk comes home
in between passing thirteen hours
blasting
the philosopher's stone he hasn't found
just sand and gravel were his daily gain
and, falling freely on his day's labour, rain.

POETRY

Excepting Poetry and me
no one was in the park.
Only someone like Poe
shows himself at dusk
under old elm trees.
I have seen Poe.
Under the elm trees he stood
in the wet leaves, alone
in dripping rain.
I saw Poe.
He wore the coat
with the velvet trim
looking sombrely for—I don't know.
Don't be a fool, Brambach! Try
a melody,
imagine a bird,
take Poe's old black bird,
let it fly . . . truly,
I have seen Poe
slowly becoming one
with the elm trees in the rain.

THE AXE

Morose after a quarrel over nothing,
obstinate both you and I, over nothing at all,
we came to this unknown village.
Dusk blended manure and milk
by the cowsheds.
We saw the farm hand at the cleaving block
under the barn roof,
saw the axe and heard it strike,
heard for a long while at our backs
the silence, the axe, the silence, the axe
striking the block.

SCHOOLYARD

The games of playtime over, the ball
forgotten in a corner and
the yard as quiet as if there was
laughter in the crown of the chestnut tree
fluttering swift as a bird.

Geraniums at the windows, as it used to be,
but long since blurred
are heart and writing, bygone names
engraved with a shard
in the plaster of the wall.

AT THE HOARDING

He and his girl
in the street, a common street
surrounded by spluttering engines
and exhaust fumes they stand

Speed rowdy leatherhead thunder arse
roaring past . . .

At the Bell Tell Shell hoarding
or something similar, very similar
and close to the abstract paintings
of old oil
on the street
they stand together
quietly
as if a weekend were close.

PAUL

For Jürg Federspiel

Born on a day below zero
in nineteen hundred and seventeen

he ran across the playground, wild,
fell, and ran on

kicking the ball across the schoolyard,
fell, and ran on

with the rifle in his hand across the training ground,
fell, and ran on

on a day below zero
into a Russian barrage

and fell.

BY THE RIVER

The river water flows as if nothing had happened
and what is rooted in the banks
stays mute.
The coot starts up, squawking,
perhaps a witness—
Its word goes unrecorded.

An under-ripple tries to spin
a maple leaf, a rotten piece of wood. Deemed too light,
they sway off—
It's not worth the effort
to raise the holed boat, only Him
they're still searching for, who sat here yesterday afternoon
and left his jacket in the willow thicket.

IT WAS LONELINESS THAT FORCED ME

On the stubblefields near Salkhofen
it was loneliness that forced me suddenly
to talk out loud, to mumble others'
poems, drifting on the dust from fields.

Crows, with weights of air in their feathers
slow in front of fir tree copses, and
chimneys in the hazy distance, fingers
pointing at busy affluence.

The path—through land as dry as Africa—
leads to the centre of the world. Oh light
and ochre heave in the ripening rye.
The Bedouins' ephemeral shadows
round the sheaf-tents I shall not forget.

IN THE AFTERNOON

This time it appeared in the afternoon
and not as usual
at night.
It has come back, but by day
I didn't have a name for it either.
This time, it seemed to be yellow.
I was sitting in the kitchen,
a burnt-down match
between my fingers.

TOSS A COIN

That metallic sound
ringing in the ear, for a few seconds,
means good luck or bad luck
or neither.

Perhaps someone is raising a glass
and speaking of you,
with no Ifs or Buts—

Across the forest
or along the clearing?
Aerial and pine tree are neighbours.
Make up your mind, it's getting dark.

If in doubt, toss a coin.
Heads or tails,
which do you choose?

LETTER TO HANS BENDER

For us the contours,
the accents.
For us the tobacco field, tall as a man,
and the vineyard in Baden.
For us the white poplar by the Rhine,
the flock of birds under the clouds,
and, as for me, everything
above the clouds too.

For you the table, the paper
and the reliable pen—
For me the axe,
I don't like weeping willows.
What kind of trees are these,
pointing downwards, Hans,
since Strasbourg travelling by my side
on this earth.

DREAMT POEM

When the toads were herbs
and the poplars horsetail—
Stay with me,
cut the bread.
Dawn only flees
to return.
Stay.

OLD PEOPLE'S HOME

As a gardener living in retirement
I still know
the timetable of all eight winds.
My forecasts
about the arrival times of the rainclouds
are reliable.

Apart from gout and the insatiable craving
for a schnapps
I have no complaints. My friends are dead
and my enemies missing.

This world which I no longer understand
calls on me in the shape of a newspaper
once a week
and several times a day
a flock of sparrows flutters to the window.

Rewarding the trust they have shown
I've elevated them to chaffinches.

LIGHT IN AUGUST

A brooding day of melancholy,
the stone lies still with inward gaze.
This world is mute. The pear tree watches
over my garden, grass and wine.

Thorny hedges show me kindness
where no sun will shine.
Weeds grow tall for me to hide in—
reddish slugs are slowly writhing,
in their midst I lie entwined.

BISTRO

Provençal summer, racing cyclists
from well to well, chasing laurels
already withered.

Provençal summer, Petrarch's sonnets
burnt with anchor and heart
into the sailor's arm.

A coat of arms with tiger lilies
a fluttering triangle of cockerels and hens,
stage, where maize grows into wheat,
wheat into grapes.

Provençal summer. Time trial
stained with red wine.

SUNG LANDSCAPE

In the schoolroom village children sing a folk song.
An ink-stained forest grows up from the desks,
a solitary clearing, a blueberry slope.
Afterwards, in the arithmetic lesson, as usual,
the reliable potato field outside the window,
while an artificial star orbits the Earth.

CONFIDENCE

One should celebrate as soon as there's occasion,
especially when all alone in a small bar,
when a poem's turned out well which may not
be liked by anyone you do not know, and warm
up your inspiration with a second bottle
again, poet and forever ne'er-do-well,
after the third bottle you have got it,
just like your heart which one day will stand still.

HIKE

Deserted peat bogs, pastures, grassy paths,
a farmyard without a watchdog,
shabby chickens behind wire mesh,
manure, just as it is and pure—
a two-armed signpost, pointing to Vögelsen
and Sankt Dionys—
spread out over all this is silence,
a soundless O—

THERE WILL BE

For Frank Geerk

Once there'll be an evening when you are alone.
Where are your friends, where have they all gone?
They're chatting, drinking without you around
and afterwards they'll seek a woman's arms.

And there you will be walking by the Rhine
that's bearing so much water, oh, if it were but wine!
under those plane trees you can meditate
and be kind to yourself for a change.

Günter is dead, Ulea's far away.
The Rhine has never told what drowned or sank.
And now for home, just one glance into the 'Golden Star',
who's sitting there alone, and writing: Frank!

As yet sunflowers are laughing, honey brown and round
apples in the grass, in the distance a lawnmower's drone
Ulea walks past the fence, earnest as she greets me
I'm overwhelmed by fear, of whom, of what?
What will be my share when the michaelmas daisies are
    here?
I'm overwhelmed by nameless fear
As yet the sunflowers are laughing, honey brown and
    round.

RICHTERSWIL II

We have the apple tree, the chestnut
and the evergreen rhododendron.
We have the roses and, more modest
but important, the kitchen herbs.
We sometimes have ourselves
and the universe above us, beyond grasping.
An ant is running across the stone table
so that I write:
an ant is running across the stone table
where I am sitting.

BRIEF NOTE

I wanted to get something dark
off my mind by writing
and I did not succeed.
If the builder has no mortar,
the stonemason no chisel,
the carpenter no wood,
we are powerless.

LE LAVANDOU

I

Many a boat has been lost to the waves
and many a sailor too.
Clouds driven by wind, an endless chase,
seagulls, sails and smoke almost blue
dispersing on the horizon's line
into tulle—
I'm sitting in the southern light,
moved like the water, and still.

II

Through the cypresses sweeps the mistral,
the palm trees bent, sand is flying.
The rocks are resting so forlorn
on the shore
and an island, never sighted,
steeped in brilliant clear blue lighting
is slowly drifting closer—
Someone like me perhaps looks out from there,
who sees the mainland coming ever nearer.

III

As the sky is overcast,
leaden and grey,
and my heart so oppressed
by what I can't say,
I am going out.
Put on your coat
which can be no more than a coat,
friends are so far—
Leave the house.

MOON

Simple things, such as milking cows,
watering begonias so they don't dry out,
diving head first, mowing the lawn,
bulging cheeks when blowing the horn,

minding the cars when crossing the road

and at night the moon as Klopstock saw it
and at night the moon as Goethe saw it
and at night the moon as Claudius saw it
and at night the moon as Hebel saw it,
to behold.

LATE MORNING

At six every day the milkman arrives
After seven the newspaper lady comes hobbling
Towards eight I come round
On the table still last night's
wine bottle and the glass, empty.
And there are the letters too
always with kind regards—
Getting up, walking around reading
Ecclesiastes eleven
'Truly the light is sweet
and a pleasant thing it is for the eyes to behold the sun . . .'

FRIENDS

This shirt that I'm wearing Willi gave me
Ulea brought the sweater one cold day
the trousers with four pockets
was Claire's gift
Werner's poetry lets me believe
The shoes are from Max
in them I'm walking towards us all the time.

↤

MERRIMENT IN THE GARDEN

Can I say: the well is welling?
Chives don't belong in a vase
even if they have purple blossoms.
Tell me—why not?
I crumble a sage leaf between my fingers,
mallows are coming up,
a regiment of ferns is rising against me.
Tipsies flower in red
and I in blue, *compostifolium brambachcensis.*

ACHIM RAABE

Nursery, glasshouses,
quarry,
paths through meadow and field.
For that is where Achim walked,
the gardener,
who provided himself with cypresses,
also wrote with a grass-green pencil,
raised his hat to boulders,
had a special fondness for Hölderlin,
would be nine now or ninety,
but—

THE WIND BEAK

Last night
the gentle wind
has on rocks and cliffs
cut its whispering tongue
to make it a beak
full of song.

By daybreak
in grey light
after wind beak's wrath
black and battered
branches were strewn
over roads and parks.

Swiftly they came
moaning with gout
old women in droves
and cleared
all the parks.

Black treasures
under aprons
shone a light,
a wrinkled
light on their faces.

SUMMER SUNDAY

Veils of silence and dust,
I hear them again and again
between the branches and foliage,
light as the feathers of birds.

Coolness from an open gate,
midday, oh mouthless humming,
ringing in my ears again
when the crickets have fallen silent.

Slowly the molehill is growing
higher in the grass,
between the wings of the window
the tension grows in the glass.

THE TREE

Since I've been living
way out in the house on the estate,
a tree is growing from the cellar
through hallway and attic.
Foliage is hanging like flags
from all windows.
The treetop is swaying
above the moss-grey roof.

I dwell unbothered close to the branches
the cleaving block rots in the yard,
the saw rusts in the attic.
The neighbours, however, call out to each other:
His house is like our houses,
how merry is the fool—
Listen, he sings at dawn, talks
and laughs as dusk falls.

The tree is growing.

DOG DAYS

Slowly the wells are running dry
The stray dogs are looking for water
The spice seller is nodding off in his shop vault
Nobody is buying pepper
Outside the knife grinder's leisurely turning his wheel
He chases the dogs away without a sound
He observes the seller
He waits
This is the time of sharpened blades.

EVIL TRICKS

He's playing evil tricks on you,
you can tell by his smile.
Crowned with a wreath,
he has not a single immaculate leaf to show
in his book.

Children, flowers and old ladies,
he loves them, they pose no danger.
But you are afraid to shout out loud,
cursing his name in the marketplace.
You want to live.

REPORT FROM THE GARDEN

With the fiery revelations
of roses
midday makes its entry into the house.
Silence descends on the dining room
for a while until
the meat is shared out
and the glasses have been emptied.

Outside the trellis casts its shadow
on the resting gardener.
He will never learn
what the walnut tree, the one that must fall
in the afternoon, leaves unsaid.

ONE DAY AMONG MANY

Geraniums are flowering
at slaughterhouse windows,
and someone who hates me
raises his hat in greeting—
At seven
the bell strikes seven, nothing more.
The night, it will
force me to the lamp.

BROODING SUMMER

Although its reign
forced straw hats upon us,
we wisely kept in the shade.
Sometimes a fire siren sounded nearby
while over Alsace
heavy clouds ponderously retreated.

No one was able to relieve
the trees of their fever fits.
Only the night made us prick up our ears,
and we acquired with ease
this one word: iceberg.

The name of salvation was Water.

IDENTITY CARD

Still quite steady on my feet
at three in the morning after celebrating
on my way home through empty streets
I was asked for an identity card
and pulled a poem, soaked with red wine,
from my pocket:
At three in the morning after celebrating
still quite steady on my feet
on my way home through empty streets—

DAY IN JULY

By the quiet reservoirs
where wind is weaving in the rushes
I can only sense and wonder
what is alive in reeds and willows.
To be a semblance of this day
the dragonfly rises abruptly
hovering on the water, sparkling:
the summer's exclamation mark.

ENCOUNTER

Sweet pea rampant among roses
and also light, falling vertically
into dried-up wells,
and later, on the garden path, I
groping my way through a dumb distant
deserted Sunday . . .
Seen in passing
shrubs and foliage and grass
looking at me with a brittle smile.

GRANITE

Stooped over granite—from southern quarries
while your hammer falls
a sky of frosted glass rising into your eyes
while your chisel hollows the groove
you taste the dust of petrified forests.

Stooped over granite—
Oh gorse and aloe slate-grey blurring
while your knee presses
against the dried-out plains
—from southern quarries
while your back, wet with sweat, is brushed
by the cool breeze of a northern summer.

✦

SANT EREMO

The bell is ringing
over the cloister
The garden
is a paradise
even without an apple tree
Life after death
no doubt
here the monastery's brandy
is golden yellow
and sweet.

UNDER APPLE TREES

Nettles grew taller than our fences
The linden trees were fragrant as ever
Now apples ripen towards their fall
Babbling tongues in the green asylum
Perhaps a barn will go up in flames
A child will drown unheard in the pond
The beekeeper laughs in veils of tulle and smoke
Babbling tongues in the green asylum
What do the apples remind us of?
And the quarry too will crumble.

TIREDNESS

For a long time already
I've been meaning to give you a name, my opponent:
You place the yoke on my neck, the sluggish
sandbag, your blunt hammer,
you make me a slave.

I carry you from the field to my evening meal,
I feel your burden
when the moon rises and the bat flies.
The others at the table call me dreamer
while my neck is bowing to you,
close to defeat.

PORTRAIT OF A YOUNG MAN

A few poetry books on the shelf in my room,
the little cheerfulness when whistling
a melody while working on sandstone and
on rainy Sundays a visit to
the public art gallery.

In a side room—little noticed—the portrait
of a young man around 1470, Upper German School,
a little boorish, perhaps a servant in the baggage train
or a stonemason.

I sat for the painter back then. Has much time passed since?
Oh, this late autumn is as frosty as it was then,
the sound of the rain
has remained unchanged,
through the midday in quarries,
summery just a while ago,
leaves are falling, pale brown.

THE ERRATIC ROCK

Rock, I'm squatting
small as a toy in front of you,
ancient mosshead with your
angular face.

The stonemason is not fond of you,
you dull his chisel,
are without ornament,
bleak patience.

Your siege, rock,
your force here—
how does the earth carry you,
solitary one, speak!

IN JULY AND AUGUST

For years, in July and August
when villas, offices, schools
and football fields are deserted,
I've received greetings every day from far away.
The postman drops
an alphorn player, Alps included,
the Bridge of Sighs, Rodin's *Thinker*,
a Serb in Turkish trousers
and also the reedy shores of a North Sea island
into my letter box.

Friends remember me
after leaving without me.

EMBASSY

It would be easy for me to describe the street,
the embassy building, flag and sign,
the rhododendron bush by the gate, also the humble
moss in the gutter.
It would be easy for me—
Here comes a briefcase,
an umbrella,
a tail coat with medal,
a fur coat,
a livery
and here comes a machine gun,
ordering me to move on.

WORDS FOR W.

My friend W., a genius
forever full of visions
but never blessed with the grace
of keeping an appointment—

This morning finally
I asked him to come yesterday evening.
He was on time.

BELATED ICARUS

My friend, the painter Sven,
builds all sorts of airships after work.
The scrapheaps on the edge of town
provide him with plenty of metal.
He's tired of modern art,
says Sven, while the swallows
excel in the evening sky.

NO ONE WILL COME

No one has come across the field.
Only rainclouds, wind.
No one will come and say:

Figure of clay, rise from the ditch,
I have heard your thoughts.
Go forth! The beautiful world awaits you!

No one will call: Hey, not on the road yet?
Your *laissez-passer* is valid,
the hand of honesty clearly legible.

As a child I saw the dancing bear
turning round and round at the fairground,
later I lay in hiding during the day,
I know a few jails inside out
and the language of the hangman.

No one. Rainclouds. Wind.

SALT

We need each other. We are
the salt of the earth,
salt, more precious than gold, more needed,
monosyllabic, white, contained in the salt cellar,
lost in the Atlantic Ocean,
in bread, in a tear, in sweat
before our birth or somehow, somewhere else
we need each other, salt of the earth.

DEATH OF A CENTAUR

After Thornton Wilder

When Shelley drowned
he was absorbed by a poem
which was to be called 'Death of a Centaur'.

On the quays of La Spezia
the dogs were sleeping as usual
in the shade of the sails,
and the sailors preparing their boats
for departure . . .

None of them saw
how that poem
hovered over the Mediterranean—
then drifted across Tyrol to the North
where Ibsen caught it and wrote down:
Master Builder Solness.

ENDANGERED LANDSCAPE

When the dove carried the olive branch,
the crack in the mountain did not matter,
the water was pure.

Apple tree in the spring time,
apple tree in the autumn,
you were as perfect
as your forefathers in paradise.

Fire in the deserted quarry.
The Gypsy gleamed here and there
but it never became clear
what he was doing.

Poppy, glowing eye of the cornfield,
for you it sufficed to know
what a corn ear looks like.

SINGLE MEN

One collects stones.

One acquires stamps.

Another one plays Tele chess

and one lurks in the evening in the park.

One learns Russian.

One reads Shakespeare.

One writes letter after letter

and one drinks red wine in the evening,

nothing else happens.

They drink, read, lurk, acquire,

the men alone in the evening.

They write, learn, play, collect,

each one to himself after work.

One goes to an operetta.

One listens to Bach.

One keeps a secret.

Like a dog on a chain, he runs down the avenues,
    every evening.

ORGANIC FAULT

Is it my eardrum? My hearing
has been tuned to a new pitch for days.
When the fish was dangling on the hook
its fearful screams shrieked towards me,
I tore up my fishing licence
and sold my fishing rod.

IRONING

Kathrin is grey haired, an elderly spinster
but still fit enough to handle
the iron all day,

oh, Kathrin, bony, without breasts,
valued as a person and appreciated
by distinguished customers—

what tender radiance
occasionally fills your eyes
when with stiff fingers

you spread out a particularly beautiful
men's shirt
on the table in front of you.

In front of you, with stiff fingers.

THE STRANGER

The one who asked me for the way
was from Greece.
Argos, Chios, Athens.
The way to the Baden Station
was difficult to explain.
I reminded him of the Odyssey.
He raised his hat, in the raindrops
dolphins glistened,
silvery.

THE END OF SOMETHING

You had laughter in your throat.
I had tears.
In the glass,
the burn mark on dirty old plush,
we sat, unremarkable.
As one sits in public.
Teafaced Salvation Army singing
oh, Father Booth, sunshine, heaven
and art nouveau cash register
off to the scrapheap—
the bar now refurbished
with wrought-iron features.

Being dead persuades through silence,
and probably you're laughing still, I
still feel tears rising, sometimes.
Not for you.

↵

VISIT IN M.

We wanted to visit the grave of the poet
and found the gate locked.
In vain the sun on our necks, we walked away
and presented our wilting gladioli
to a beauty walking past, laughing.

SETTING SAIL

When the ropes are untied
when the gangway's pulled in
seagulls and hands flutter up
on board
hands and seagulls flutter up
on the quay
and the air is set in motion
by hands and seagulls,
and at the stern
water is moving and frothing
and on the faces
on board and on the quay
as always
that special something appears
which has nothing
to do with water and air.

SOUTHERN TOWN

Inhabited by the sun,
towers, roofs, squares and fountains,
while the shade
settles in the lanes.

The girls of this town
walk from
sun to shade to sun
I among them,
a poet, a man.

THE GINGKO LEAF

The moss covered idler, sandstone, matt,
the castle ridge, long since humbly hill-bent,
above the town it flies its rag.

Battered wet by ricochet rain,
the asphalt glistens in black velvet richness,
on wings of leaves the avenue sways.

There sails the sign, the leaf of the gingko
from the tree towards the strip of grass,
destined for you, tenderly: Take it, there lingers
still the air, the touch of a summer to last.

←

POEM FOR FRANK

Don't give in, ever
because everything gives way—
So much yellow in the air,
gossip squatting in the stench.

We want to talk green
like the tree, the bush,
the grass, simple and
ever returning,
year by year.

YOU BESIDE ME

As you're walking beside me, cheerful,
praising this working day as a Sunday,
picking up a shiny pebble
by the wayside,
tell me! How shall I comfort you
as a snail shell
cracks under my foot—you
gently ensconced
in this midday of Indian Summer . . .

COMING HOME

The axe on my shoulder, I'm trotting
home, in the cold hand of wintery silence,
want to hang tiredness,
a grey weight of lead,
up in the branches carelessly,
want to make my entry into your room,
throwing my hat in the air, whistling.

And suddenly I remember
one summer, some time,
your fair hair, the slope of rye,
poppies and pouting lip . . .

The axe on my shoulder, I trot.
Transformed the hill, a listless sack of flour,
a snowy sky descends to cover it in snow,
The lamp receives me with its morose light.

A LEAF IN MEMORY OF SEPTEMBER

Who said that birds' word
was September which will not return?
Now I'm in May. The midday light
vibrates on the windowpane.
Along with the smell of camphor,
dried leaves in the Old Testament,
the missing autumn
rises once more from the chest.

What I did not believe you
didn't want to know.

←

HARD TIMES FOR DRINKERS

Potatoes in the basket,
a string of onions dangling
but the Beaujolais's been battered by hail,
and Burgundy's covered in frost.

Since the plover
has come in droves to settle,
I've called out to my friends:
Dry times are coming!

To each child her doll,
oats aplenty for the stiff-necked donkey,
for us but chalk and stone
for a game of hopscotch . . .

and a taste of vinegar on the tongue.

BACK THEN

Back then when we were gaping
at strange names
like Amilcar, Bugatti, Ford and Studebaker,
spelling them out,
the coachmen were on their way
into the museum.
Those were also the times
when we, at dusk
under the gas lamps,
had a different illumination.

IN THE VINEYARD

A gentle blue is weaving
through the vineyard again.
Go there before the harvest begins,
lie back, and soon you are
a peaceful neighbour to grapes and leaves.

Rest.
The vine grows gradually,
the grape ripens slowly under the leaf, and
nobody spurs you on—he is silent,
the other, the drifter in fetters,
who rises up inside you,
who is always with you, who calls you—
he's silent.

GOODBYE TO THE EIFEL

The house has been cleared
the house has dreamt its dream
dog kennel and children's stuff
axe, shovel, whetting stone, butt
given away, sold or lent out—
I am free to go down south.

The leaves are already turning
the starlings have left on their journey
I've paid my visit one last time
The priest shall read another Mass
And I will drink just one more glass
Village children will wave goodbye.

SHOTS

Beautiful autumn forest! Say father and mother.
Autumn forest, silence of berries, silence of grass—
in a clearing the gleam of metal
aimed at traces of flight.
Beautiful autumn forest! The children call.
Where shots fall words don't count.
Not in a clearing
nor anywhere else.
This leaf the red colour of blood! Cries the mother.
Let's take it home with us, says the father.

PROMENADE

Promenade green, stirring.
Stay there for a while,
promenade green is soothing
to the eyes and,
according to some colour theories,
to your heart.

You are not alone. The poet
stands, ivy round his shoe,
on his plinth—
a darker green, now cleansed
by the rain, it shines.
Different shades
bundled
into green as such
and yet the wind runs through it
and stirs it.

BEYOND RIJEKA

The field belongs to whom
and who has fenced it in
and why?

This barbed wire
extra strong,
behind it grass grows
that belongs to the earth
and to whom belongs this earth?

Sheep grazing here—
I don't know,
I don't understand Croatian—
Without shepherd or dog
sheep grazing here and there.

BLACK FOREST

Surrounded by tree trunks
unmarked,
leave the cuckoo to its clock,
look for a shingle roof.
Tree bark, pine cones and needles
are dry proof to you:
you're in a blind alley of the woods.

ATHLETICS FOR HARES

My name is Bunny.
They call me Longears too,
the great sprinter.
My hare heart trembles
as the gunshot roars
across the track in the field—
Ready steady go into the yonder.

HEALTH

I know the Louvre only from the outside
and the Eiffel Tower from below.
A walk by the Seine, then into a bistro.
At the table I raised my glass: Santé!
I think I sat there just a little bit too long.
What happened after the eighth glass—
I deny it.
The Prison de Paris is called Santé.

LUCKY CHARMS

Who'd be surprised that the cats
turned shy and the dog vicious?
Four-leaf clover is just cattle feed,
even the child in the house knows that.
And the horseshoe at the stable door
belonged to the old farm horse
who keeled over and died, and that is all.

DEPARTURE

Watching through the bull's eye of the cabin
how the dunes are drifting imperceptibly—
your hope to be a witness to the changes,
and your wish to see the new map
already printed,
while the ship's band, seasick
from goodbyes,
grows ever older during the waltz.

Count your luggage—the fish
can stay outside—
Count as Noah counted once before.

LATE IN THE EVENING

My songbird flew away.
Wherever I listen
there is no one
to praise this evening.

The conversation next door
or loud laughter
cannot deceive me
as the evening slowly grows shorter.

In an hour or two
we will engage with this silence
together and alone,
between wall, wall and wall . . .

Wherever I listen,
my songbird is dead.
A biting frost sharpens
the white crescent above us.

COLD

The michaelmas daisy market has faded
In the late afternoon its blue appeared
once more above the roofs.
When night fell
the curious junk-shop owner was seized
by fear of dying
He touched his furniture . . . never
had it seemed so worn to him . . .
later the shrill shop bell went
and the cold moved in
as no one pulled the door shut.

TRACES

Rainwater in potholes
Blown-up bunker
Molehill
Ashes after the blaze
Bird droppings—

Not worth a mention, you say,
lets talk about us and the ants
before we go away,
for ever.

DARK DAY

Smoke drifting off. What does the bell ring?
The hour late
does not differ
from the hour early.
The people on their way
lower their heads
as if ashamed
that the trees are naked.
A little brightness could be
found only in jolly children's books
if it wasn't for the little Sicilian now
arriving with his vocal music of summer
and his blood oranges.

FLIGHT TIME

Leaves are falling, empty
birds' nests are showing in the branches.
It rains and goes on raining
until there's snow—
There'll be a day which will coldly
blow November on foghorns,
and huddled to our chins
in wool we'll stand and check our roofs.
The holes we'll fill with worry.
It would be time to fly.

STRAW FLOWERS AS FAREWELL

You rolled up the market parasol,
carried away the baskets for fruit,
your voice
which had been calling out summer for long
fell silent.

Above the bare branches,
as winter will have it,
there is the noise of gulls and crows,
while you in your glasshouse
are silently tying straw flowers in bundles.

As night falls earlier with every day
what else is there for me to gain
but the essence of dust
from the flower you gave me.

PIGEONS WHEN SLEEP IS ALL I LONG FOR

Pigeons, will you leave the rooftop
to flutter into waiting hands?
No salt nor flour in the earthen bottles,
windswept by winter lies my land.

Pigeons, will you heed me calling
or will you fly into your loft?
If pigeons on the roof were frozen
who knows what else might be our lot?

Watch out for traces thin as cobwebs,
for snares set out beneath the snow!
The season works its evil forces,
if I'll resist—I do not know.

Pigeons, when sleep is all I long for
then hunger bites, keeps me awake.
The miserere has been sung now,
but for the snow the roof is bare.

HOTEL ROOM

When you move out, throw
your memories into the bin
with blotting paper and envelope.

Restless patrons have carried
away the colours from the carpet
and the pale flowers on the wallpaper—
what remains
is a blurred grey in the mirror.

Pack your travelling bag.
In the lobby—you have already
forgotten the number on your key—
the revolving door is spinning in the wind
from countries as yet unexplored.

CAUTION SHOULD BE CALLED FOR

What pushes you to write poetry?
Why don't you peddle salt,
houses, shotguns or tobacco?

Caution should be called for, you know it, for soon
the ravens will come back—black preachers
without oil in their voices—to cry out
your poverty,
while you are still walking around unfazed.

When icicles are hanging from the well
you have the station waiting room as your abode
where, echoing in many tongues,
departure and arrival mingle.

EVERYDAY

Going where I have to go
Planting a young tree
Praising the garden even if it rains for long
Oiling the wheel
and checking the brakes.
Reading the newspaper without wanting to emigrate
Welcoming friends
Being able to forget
Roses or chicken?
Writing poems and
not listening to
the double bass music in the sky
which is cloudy or blue.

Also in April

For Ulea

A stone-hard poem
  full of bumpy lines

The year still young. I'm seized by a boisterous mood,
rainwater vat rhymes with sunshine in March
warming my back
and drying the moss-covered stone bench—
This springtime too will bring me by the by
plenty of quiet work round the garden.
What else?
Patience, Rainer, patience.

No sweet green glade,
a workshop and yard—
not my father's house,
a shed—
If someone's looking for me,
I'm with Kurt, the stonemason.
We share our lunch break,
squinting health into the sunshine
surrounded by a load
of granite, lime and sandstone.

As it has been raining for three days
a quiet steady rain
I take my three colour pencils
blue yellow and green
and draw a sky
a sun in it
and underneath a dandelion meadow
on paper—
The red stain on the meadow—
spilt wine.

My ancestors never left the north behind,
nor did my father and mother.
Perhaps they begot me,
so I would come here
to these hills of oak tree and vine
to this wild rocky land of cypresses
to the juniper gorse and olive-tree country.

Covered in dust and thirsty I squat on a stone
and tell myself: this country
is a stone-hard poem full of bumpy lines,
the smell of oil, brown wine,
of thorns, eyes of leather brooding in silence
until the wind rises that makes the olive branches
tremble in silvery hues.

So many wonders in this world
for baffled mankind to behold,
Doctor Eisenbart for example
was a healer after his own manner:
He made blind people clearly see,
and lame men walk on their own feet,
but only on the first of April
always only on the first of April.

Dust is still an alien word.
The meadows wet, the fields
dark brown, heavy and damp,
but your warm hand, Ulea,
weighs gently in mine
as we wander—our motto is patience—
through the shifting lightning,
the April light.

The ribbon blue as Mörike saw it
fluttering in the air—but where?
I see a vapour trail
drawn across the sky—
the blackbird though is always there at dusk
on the rooftop opposite, singing its song,
unspeakable—

←

The maypoles standing tall
in the villages along the Upper Rhine
hung with colourful ribbons—
so much confidence for the days
between the eleventh and the fifteenth of May!
Mamertus,
Servatius, Boniface, Pancras,
the grumpy, frosty saints are due
followed by Cold Sophie
haggard and frigid
at night with her quicksilver heart
mostly below zero.

Not strange at all: inside me whinnies a horse,
inside me crows a cockerel!
Stretching, arriving, waking up,
tearing off yesterday's calendar leaf
to read the proverb on the back
and forget it,
bidding a good May morning to the lime tree in the yard
and opening the window wide.

The birds are shouting it from the rooftops:
This is where the tenth spring poem should be,
the poet wrote it at night over some wine
and then it got misplaced or lost—
Shut up now, birds! I'll seek and I'll find,
perhaps it got caught in a bush of thorns.

Two flitting cabbage whites
spinning a yarn

The evening's still far away. The sun
won't think of waning—
What on earth happened to
Veronica's veil? Amen.
In front of me the cornfield, the stalks
higher than a man,
the hollyhocks just as big.
Sheep, sleeping in the shade, village children.
A farmhand gaping
by the gate of the barn,
two flitting cabbage whites spinning a yarn—
the sundial on the church tower crumbling.
Topinambour.
On the horizon
a cumulus cloud hill rising tall,
and I, between cornstalks and hollyhocks,
so small.

Your strength Ulea
being able to sleep
before midnight
and my weakness
being unable to sleep
before midnight—
Venus above
the Plough
Mars and Moon
and as the curtain billows
in a soft breeze
the clock ticks
the heart beats
and someone Ulea sits at the table
looking for an ending
that will take him to bed gently.

A stiff old-fashioned straw hat
on his nut (as he would always call his head),
my father Franz Philip Brambach
used to sit in a beer garden
on summer evenings
a pint of lager on the tin table in front of him—
Franz, born in 1859 in Rheinbach near Bonn,
tired of Wilhelmine German sabre rattling
arrived in Basel in 1908
and, thanks to the beer garden
on Langen Erlen street, that's where he stayed.
His straw hat, bearing the stamp
of the sun through June, July and August,
gave Franz the piano tuner
an enormous dignity, in particular
when he was wearing his tailcoat
and his rubber collar, cleansed with pure petrol.

Recently, as I was tidying up in the attic,
a tuning fork and Franz's straw hat quite simply
got out of a suitcase into my hands—
I put the hat on my head, went out
and took it, and also the fork in my pocket,
under the leafy roof of a beer garden
in vaguely melancholy mood.

←

High noon, Sunday afternoon
The quiet gardens
behind hedges of boxtree and hornbeam
the deserted suburban streets—
Standing at a bus stop
I see the heat like flickering glass
on the road surface
and enchanted I hear
where from, now, where from
Debussy's *Prélude à l'après-midi d'un faune.*

Me with my prose,
me with my poetry
and otherwise also just me—
But these granite stairs,
these twelve steps,
the limestone joists
and the dry stone wall,
a double wall, waist-high—
some twenty years ago
I built it.
I was a garden builder,
I made things that last.

Perpetual begetting in the rural idyll,
the he-goat mounts the she-goat,
the cockerel mounts the hen—
The whitish light. The silent midday.
Smell of tobacco on the threshing floor.
From the Jura a relieving storm draws nearer—
suddenly the cat comes dashing past.
The little bird—she didn't catch it after all.
Meanwhile the heavy rain is drumming
already on the hot roof tiles.

Summer evenings in the Sankt Johann quarter
the brass band's concert in the park
horse droppings lying in the street
good fertilizer for allotments.
There were bats back then,
always swift, chasing after midges,
and couples on the benches under trees.
That was July and August in the Sankt Johann quarter
and sometimes a soft melody
on the ocarina.

Not wanting to be part of it sometimes
making off into the underwood
past many a silly cow—
Then, lying in the elder shade, timeless,
not giving a damn
if one and one are three.

Concrete can be so ugly—
I can tell from the blown-up bunkers
along the Rhine.
The castle above the valley, however,
abandoned centuries ago
a romantic ruin—
I'm sitting on a ledge
dangling my feet
I, the minstrel, and beside me
my Ulea, the damsel.

←

Surely the summer has other names
not just summer.
For instance Ulea, a name
combining corn yellow, rye red,
meadow and forest green
in one.

The words: Terror tender touching Titian Red
written in my notebook.

To live in a sunflower
honey brown
in alliance
with meadow saffron forever autumnal.
To gather oneself, sunny
for winter is coming
that ice-cold baldhead.

Fly a kite
call it October
A handful of walnuts in Wollbach
In Mauchen a fair bit of wine from the wood
the line: 'Whoever has no house now will establish none'
the line: 'Whoever lives alone now will live on long alone'
the dahlias the michaelmas daisies
predominantly blue
is the afternoon's yield.

To write a poem
without ballast
for instance late autumn
empty snail shell cobwebs
something falling silently
amid the whispers of the trees.

Month of wine an old calendar word
written into my notebook
the vines on the South slope
the daytime moon a grey piece of earthenware
a partridge starting up and wooden silence.
The words Terror tender touching Titian Red
written in my notebook
Libra and Scorpio.

Westwind with its unspeakable force
tears through the cypresses
swirling up leaves on
stone, the inscription
Siste Viator et lege, hic jacet—
wind from the Vosges
and a lifeless green
over the graves.

Taking a bite from an apple or pear
along the field path
giving praise to this day
kindly and cool—
This blackbird blackness in that girl's gaze
plain melody of autumn sung by a crow
and ever closer
the Hirschen, the Krone, the Rebstock,
their hospitable rooms
where I pay a visit to myself.

The rows of vines form lightless lines

a mouse-grey something flits noiselessly across the
    ploughed field

my harmonica stays in my pocket

I owe an answer to all questions

all I can say is: perhaps—

Day without sun, day that belongs to water.

The cottage gardens come up with their cabbage
the last wallflowers grow pale
the plump peasant woman with her windfall fruit
and a frowning poplar crowned with a crow's nest.
Fly your paper swallow on the wind, young friend,
for as long as you will, the buzzard
flies higher and more venerably still.

Last day of October. Take your rucksack
and wander once again the familiar paths.
The boundary stone in the grass, granite permanence
the rough-hewn bench by the edge of the woods, sit down
look up to the pastel-coloured sky,
Hölderlin's lines: 'But
lovely it is to unfold
the soul and our brief life—'

Free time working time dinner time
and the time to sleep—
The fast trains the slow trains
the coming and the going—
Early November and yet it seems
I heard the cuckoo just a little while ago.

Ice grey, a wolf word, a winter word
panted into the hoarfrost—

Must a summer poem be bright,
an autumn poem be quiet,
a winter poem be white?

I ask. I'm being snowed under by snow.
The path but a faint trace, I'm alone,
as the saying goes, alone as a stone—
My footsteps—snow is wiping them out.
A consuming desire burns inside me:
a shot of rum in steaming hot tea.

Sitting by the window I observe
in the snow-covered garden
black tomcat Stanislaus who lives next door.
He walks with care, hesitates
and looks back again and again—

and looks back as if thinking:
What happened to old cosiness,
what is this ice-cold rug about!
Stanislaus proves to me, black on white,
what cats are like, what just all cats are like.

A postcard from the Caribbean
taken out of the letter box—
oh well, Caribbean,
while I—all blessings come from Heaven above—
have a white Black Forest in front of me.

Ice grey, a wolf word, a winter word
panted into the hoarfrost—
The windblown haystack in the field
in front of the forest
and above the forest drifting smoke
and above the smoke the Vosges Mountains—and
how freezing cold they must have been
Poilu Jean and Private Fritz in their foxholes
during a lull in the battle
back then by Hartmannsweiler.

My four and sixtieth winter.
How often snow has fallen since!
As little lads, Kurt, Paul and I,
peed our initials yellow into the white—
I with a flourish: R B

Rust-red Reynard, whither now?
Nagging hunger drives you about—
I've seen your tracks in the snow, listen:
Perhaps it was me who stole the goose,
the door of the pen is open, brittle and mute.

Picked up a handful of snow and compressed it
and hurled the ball—a raven flies up,
sending a raven black curse
across the snowblown path snowballs snowberries
when are the snowberries ripe after all
consider it now, at the end of December—

Ten degrees below zero
and again a hearty
sneeze into the handkerchief
wiping my watering eyes
and skipping and hopping
until the ice puddle cracks
and a delicate spinet rings
persistently in my ears—

Foehn wind in February
The peaks of Blauen and Belchen appear within reach
The wilful wind
a quarrelsome voice—
Now snowmen are melting
weathercocks and wind vanes going crazy—
Knife, rope and matches
the landscape sways in a fever
through me and my headache.

Never put to paper and yet unforgotten
the soft light of the gas lamps in the evening
the snowball fights won and lost
the downhill races on the wooden sledge
the roast hot chestnuts
in the newspaper cone
and the Hoorays in thoughtless songs.
Beauty of our childhood years, they won't come back.

Notes

p. 19, 'Letter to Hans Bender'

accents: in German, *Akzente* refers to the German literary periodical which Hans Bender edited for many years. Bender discovered Rainer Brambach as a poet and published a number of his poems in *Akzente*.

p. 106, 'My ancestors never left . . .'

Siepi, Tuscany, end of March, dedicated to Ruedi Bettschart.

p. 109, 'The ribbon blue as Mörike saw it . . .'

Eduard Mörike, German poet, 1804–75, whose most famous poem is about spring and its 'ribbon blue' fluttering in the air.

p. 110, 'The maypoles standing tall . . .'

These five saints, the 'Ice Saints', are commemorated between 11 and 15 May, a period that frequently coincides with the last cold spell and frosty nights.

p. 128, 'Fly a kite . . .'

Quotes from Rainer Maria Rilke, 'Autumn Day' in *Reading Rilke, Reflections on the Problem of Translation* (William Gass trans.) (New York, NY: Alfred A. Knopf, 1999), p. 35.

p. 132, 'Taking a bite . . .'

The Hirschen, the Krone and the Rebstock are names of country inns frequented by the poet.

p. 135, 'Last day of October . . .'

From Friedrich Hölderlin, 'When there's a flaming above the vineyard' in *Selected Poems and Fragments* (Michael Hamburger trans.) (London and New York: Penguin, 2007), pp. 312–13.